EUGENIO PUCCI

ALL VENICE

IN 140 COLOR PHOTOGRAPHS

Translated by
NANCY WOLFERS MAZZONI

CHARLES SCRIBNER'S SONS
NEW YORK

A - 2. 72 (I)

Printed in Italy

Library of Congress Catalog Card Number 78 - 38889

SBN 684 - 12883-7

VENICE

With a splendid sequence of photographs in color, we present you with a detailed image of the incomparable city of Venice; a city unique not only for its infinite artistic beauties, but also for its urbanistic structure which continuously speaks a language all its own. Venice is anchored to its history which began with the decline of the Roman Empire of the West and the barbaric invasions. The barbarians, bringing destruction to the inhabited sections of the land, forced many populations to seek refuge on the numerous islands of the lagoon. It was in this way that the refugees of Aquileia, Altino and Padova began the first urbanistic center in the zone of Rialto. They proceeded to open up a thick network of canals consolidating the insular terrain. For this enormous project an intelligent town-planning scheme was adopted. The impressive Grand Canal took form as well as the numerous smaller canals of the city. Altogether, they have more than four hundred bridges connecting the one hundred and eighteen small islands which make up the whole urban agglomerate.

A thick structure of piling with large long tree trunks reinforced the islands making possible the construction of houses, palaces, and churches. These buildings constitute a living testimony of the power achieved by the Venetians in their sea-trade and territorial conquests. With the art of diplomacy

and military action they knew how to defend their conquests and the survival of the Republic.

With the passing of centuries, the actual city was formed. It is a true masterpiece of the intelligence and industry of man; a city which must be seen, because not even the most thorough descriptions can give us a concrete evaluation. Only after having known it directly, after having gone through its characteristic canals, squares, and « campielli » (small squares), and through its narrow winding streets, only then can we understand why Venice is known as one of the most unusual wonders of the world.

To the unique topographical formation must be added the ingenious contributions of innumerable artists who were able to create around the suggestive natural beauty a myriad of large and small masterpieces of architecture, sculpture and painting. They have made Venice an indispensable stopping-off place for artists, writers, poets, scholars, and cultured people. Without knowing Venice one can not pretend to have a complete knowledge of the fascinating artistic and cultural history of Italy.

The charming vision of palaces along the Grand Canal, and of churches and historical buildings in the various districts of the city present us with an impression of several artistic periods; so, as the gondola or steamer slowly makes its way along the canals, we come across the magnificent byzantine style,

A view of the exciting **historical regatta** which takes place the first Sunday of every September.

the religious romanesque style, the flamboyant gothic, the pure renaissance, and the unrestrained and spectacular baroque. As one can see, there isn't an artistic expression which Venice has rejected. But what surprises us even more is the flowering of the minor arts which has a solid tradition in every branch of artistic handicraft.

All this is not limited only to the sparkling splendour of the Grand Canal, but we find it everywhere. It may be said that there isn't a place in the vast territory of the city which hasn't been touched by the magic wand of the creative genius of various artists. The power of this presence can only be understood when we realize that the entire urban agglomerate covers an area of 7,062 square kilometers, while its perimeter, including the islands of Marittima Station, San Giorgio, St. Elena and the Giudecca, measures 13,700 kilometers.

ARRIVAL IN VENICE. - One can reach Venice by sea, by automobile, and by train. Here is a view of the parking terminal in the large **Piazzale Roma.** We arrive here by driving along the Ponte della Libertà which was built alongside the railroad in 1933. The huge garage is also a point of departure for the motor-buses that link the city to others on dry land. From the **Fondamenta di S. Croce,** a small steamer will carry us to St. Mark's Square by way of the Grand Canal. It takes about thirty minutes to make the trip.

This is a view of the busy **railroad station** constructed in 1954. A long bridge connects it to the mainland. For the construction of this bridge, which was opened in 1846, seventy-five thousand piles were sunken into the lagoon. The station is called Santa Lucia after a church dedicated to this saint which once stood in this very spot.

Leaving the station we find ourselves immediately in front of the beginning of the **Grand Canal** where steamers and gondolas are ready to accompany us to the heart of the city. They travel along this wide waterway past the splendid homes of the old Venetian nobility.

THE GRAND CANAL

Here, we see an ample view of a stretch of the Grand Canal. This marvellous undulating thoroughfare, seen from above, has the form of an upside down « S » and divides the city in two parts. It is 3,800 meters long, varies in width from thirty to seventy meters, and is five to 5.30 meters in depth. To really enjoy the Grand Canal, it is necessary to travel it by gondola because only in this way is it possible to admire, in all their particular splendour, the large and small canals, the palaces, and the squares, all of which display an ever-present beauty in all seasons of the year.

For cultivated persons both banks of the canal stir up memories of history, art, and literature. For others the trip along the canal offers an unrepeatable emotional experience for its incomparable scenery. Its ever-changing landscape, created by the sun and clouds, by the rain and by the impetuousness of the sea, by vegetation and by the multiform sequence of houses and palaces, has that unreal and evocative atmosphere that no other city in the world is able to duplicate.

Across the Grand Canal from the station, the tourist's attention is drawn to the **Church of San Simeone and Giud**a, called little San Simeone with its charming copper dome in a lively green color. It was founded in the nineth century, however, the actual construction was realized between 1718 and 1738. Inspired by the Pantheon in Rome, the interior has a circular plan. Giovanni Scalfurotto was the architect.

The Bridge of the Scalzi. - Going towards St. Mark's Square, this is the first bridge we come to. At one time, it was built of iron, but in 1933 the architect E. Miozzi designed the bridge we see here.

The beautiful church, **Santa Maria di Nazareth**, also called **degli Scalzi**, was built between 1660 and 1689. It was designed by Baldassarre Longhena. The rich façade, work of Giuseppe Sardi, is a unique example of the Venetian baroque style which was inspired by classical forms. In the interior, we find the tomb of the last Doge of Venice, Lodovico Manin.

The picturesque **Church of San Geremia** first rose in the eleventh century but it was reconstructed in the eighteenth century. Here the body of the martyr from Siracusa, Santa Lucia, is kept. The tall romanesque bell tower is one of the oldest in Venice. Beside it is the Labia Palace which is covered by a temporary fencing while it is being restored. To the left is the seventeenth century Flangini Palace by the architect Giuseppe Sardi.

The Turkish Storehouse. - In the past it was the headquarters of oriental merchants. It is constructed in the Venetian-byzantine style of the thirteenth century, reminiscent of the architecture of the Ducal Palace. The Civic Museum of Natural History now occupies the interior of the building.

CA' PESARO. - This imposing and magnificent Venetian palace in the baroque style is a masterpiece by the architect Baldassarre Longhena (1679-1710). It now houses the Collection of Oriental Art and the International Gallery of Modern Art.

In front of Ca' Pesaro, on the opposite bank of the canal, there is a fine series of typical Venetian palaces. From left to right: the **Ruoda Palace** of the seventeenth century; then, the **Gussoni Grimani della Vida Palace** of the sixteenth century probably designed by Michele Sanmicheli; beside the Noale Canal, the smaller **Da Lezze Palace**, the **Boldù Palace**, and the **Contarini-Pisani Palace**, all of the seventeenth century.

CA' D'ORO is in the magnificent Venetian style of the fifteenth century. Its name (house of gold) derives from the gilding which decorated its façade in the past. The nobleman Marin Contarini employed Bartolomeo Bon and Matteo Raverti (1421-40) to carry out this work. The Baron Giorgio Franchetti, last owner of the palace, donated it to the State along with its art collection which still carries his name.

In the foreground the **Pescheria** (fish market), built in 1907 in the Venetian gothic style of the fifteenth century by architects C. Laurenti and D. Rupolo. Since the fourteenth century the fish market has always been in this spot. In front of the Pescheria, and just behind the lantern in the photograph, is the **Michiel Palace of the Columns** so-called for its ground-level portico.

The **New Constructions of the Rialto,** a minor work by Jacopo Tatti known as Sansavino (1555). It is now the seat of the Law Courts.

The **Old Constructions of the Rialto** date from the first half of the sixteenth century, work of the architect A. Abbondi known as Scarpagnino. Here we find the vegetable market.

(Above) To the right the **German Storehouse** so-called because German merchants met here to trade their goods and buy those coming from the Orient. The architecture is by Scarpagnino (1508). Now the building is occupied by the Central Post Office. After the Rio del Fondaco there are several other typical palaces in the Venetian style. (Below) **The Rialto Bridge.**

THE RIALTO BRIDGE. - Michelangelo and Palladio participated in the competition for the construction of this bridge, but the Venetian Republic preferred this bold solution by Antonio da Ponte. He designed the bridge between 1588 and 1591, using a single arcade. Later on, some shops were added. The bridge is 48 meters long, 22 meters wide and 7.50 meters high. (Above) A charming view of the area around the bridge. On the right the Riva del Carbon (bank of coal) and on the left the Riva del Vin (bank of wine).

CA' FOSCARI. - This is the most perfect example of Venetian-gothic architecture. The Doge, Francesco Foscari, who guided the political and social life of the Republic for more than thirty years, is responsible for its construction. Many famous people have been received in this palace, among them King Henry III of France who stayed there in 1574. At present, it belongs to the Institute of Economics and Commerce of the University.

THE GRASSI PALACE. - An imposing structure in the classical style of the eighteenth century by the architect Giuseppe Massari. The Grassi family, originally from Bologna, entered the Venetian nobility in 1718. The palace is now occupied by the International Center of Arts and Costumes.

22

Ca' Rezzonico and **Academy Bridge.** - A beautiful seventeenth century palace in the baroque style designed by the architect Baldassarre Longhena. The top storey was added in the eighteenth century by Giorgio Massari. The Academy Bridge with a single arch completely in wood (1932), leads to the Academy Gallery, the principal museum of Venice which contains the masterpieces of Venetian painting.

The **Cavalli Franchetti Palace** is one of the most beautiful examples of gothic architecture of the fifteenth century. The decoration of the façade recalls the open gallery of the Ducal Palace.

CA' GRANDE. - The Corner Palace called Ca' Grande (large house) because of the imposing size of its construction is by the Florentine architect Jacopo Tatti known as Sansovino. Each element of the classical façade recalls the traditional architecture of the Venetian house. The powerful and wealthy family Corner lived here until the beginning of the nineteenth century. Now, the palace is owned by the government and occupied by the Prefecture and Administration of the Province.

SANTA MARIA DELLA SALUTE. - Near St. Mark's Square, on the right bank of the Grand Canal, the beautiful **Church of Santa Maria della Salute** may be admired by visitors. It is a masterpiece in the baroque style by the architect Baldassarre Longhena. The building has an octagonal plan and is surmounted by a dome. The construction was begun following a decree by the Venetian Senate on October 22, 1630 to give thanks to the Virgin Mary for the end of the plague which had done away with forty-seven thousand victims. The imposing and fanciful white structure has attracted the sensibilities of artists of all times who have immortalized it in their paintings and engravings.

One of the picturesque and characteristic angles which can be seen along the Grand Canal.

We have arrived at the end of the Grand Canal in the proximity of **St. Mark's Square.** Therefore, we shall leave the steamer or the gondola and give one last look at the **Church of Santa Maria della Salute.** Our eyes pass over the extensive coastline of **St. Mark's Basin**; on the right the **Giudecca Canal**, and in front of us the splendid **Island of San Giorgio Maggiore** with its beautiful church by Palladio. We can hear the lively movement of traffic of the motor-boats and steamers that connect the city with the various islands and the Lido. On the left one follows the curvilinear shoreline of the city which from **St. Mark's Wharf** leads to the ship-yard, to the **International Biennale of Art**, and to the **Naval College.** It is a long walk full of pleasant surprises, views of art, and historical sights which no one should neglect to see.

ST. MARK'S PIAZZETTA (small square). - Having gotten off the steamer at St. Mark's Wharf, we pass in front of a small fifteenth century palace in Lombard style which is the harbour office; then, we pass the small garden of the Royal Palace and the Palace of the Zecca by Sansovino. All of a sudden we find ourselves in the splendid small square which is the entrance-way to subsequent St. Mark's Square. On the left we see the most beautiful renaissance building in the city, designed by the Florentine architect Jacopo Tatti or Sansovino in 1535. This magnificent structure is the seat of the **Marciana Library.** In the background a side view of **St. Mark's Basilica** and on the right a façade of the Ducal Palace. At the far limits of this square are two robust red granite columns which come from the Orient. They were placed here in 1172 by Niccolò Barattieri. The left-hand column is surmounted by a **statue of San Teodoro**, the first protector of the Venetians. The right-hand column has a bronze statue of the **Lion of St. Mark.** This statue, which comes from the Orient, is a symbol of St. Mark the Evangelist and of the power of the Venetian Republic. Between these two columns, those condemned to death were once publicly executed.

ST. MARK'S SQUARE

A marvellous, vast open-air hall for the Venetians. The political, social and religious life of the city takes place here today as it did in the past. In this square, the echo of all the great events in which the glorious Republic played a major part, is synthesized into an harmonious framework. In the shape of a trapezoid, the great square is 175 meters and a half long, 82 meters wide on the side of the basilica, and 57 meters wide on the opposite side. The layout of the Euganean trachyte pavement and the design of the white bands was planned by the architect Andrea Tirali in 1723. In antique times the surface of the square was called « Morso » (morsel) because of the nature of the terrain which was more solid than anywhere else. A canal flowed across the square which was surrounded by trees.

31

St. Mark's Square: Above) On the left the **New Procuratie** (residence of the Procurators of St. Mark), a classical work by Vincenzo Scamozzi (1584); in the background the **Napoleonic Wing** in a neoclassic style by the architect Giuseppe Soli (1807). (Below) The **Old Procuratie** built between 1400 and 1500, perhaps the work of Codussi.

A beautiful shot of the Clock Tower built by Mauro Codussi between 1496 and 1499.

THE CLOCK TOWER. - A view of the terminal part of the tower with the bell and two « Moors » so-called because of the dark patina of their bronze. They have been striking the hours of the day for more than four centuries. They were fused into bronze in 1497 by Ambrogio de la Anchore. To the right we see the same tower with the **Winged Lion**, the emblem of Venice. Beneath it are the **Virgin and Child** in gilded copper and fifteenth century designs in relief by the sculptor and goldsmith Alessandro Leopardi. In front of the Madonna there is a small semi-circular terrace and two small doors at the sides. During the week of Ascension Day, the three « Wise Men » or Magi preceded by an angel come out of one door and reenter the other, every time the clock strikes the hour. When they pass in front of the Virgin they kneel.

The thick **mass of pigeons in St. Mark's Square** offer a cheerful welcome to tourists from all over the world. An ancient legend tells us that the pigeons were brought to Venice from the Island of Cypress to pay homage to the wife of the Doge. However, they are considered a real traditional ornament of the square, and the Commune provides for them by distributing an abundant supply of corn twice a day.

ST. MARK'S BELL TOWER. - Photographed here between Sansovino's Library and the corner of the Ducal Palace, we see **St. Mark's Bell Tower.** It is identical to the original one which was built on a Roman foundation between 888 and 912, and which collapsed on July 14, 1902. The new bell tower, the « paron de casa » (master of the house) as the Venetians call it, was inaugurated in 1912 during St. Mark's Day, since he is the protector of the city. It is 98.60 meters high and from the top one can have an enchanting view of Venice and the Lagoon. At the peak of the tower a gilded angel moves according to the way the wind is blowing.

At the foot of the bell tower the small Renaissance **loggia** by Sansovino. It was built between 1537 and 1549. The four statues which embellish it, also by the same artist, represent Apollo, Mercury, Peace, and Minerva in reference to the virtues which the Venetian Republic had held in such high esteem. When the bell tower collapsed it also shattered the loggia, which it was possible to reassemble completely with the materials recovered. In antiquity the loggia was used by the Armed Guard of the Republic to protect the sessions of the Major Council.

Two shots of the city taken from the top of the bell tower: (above) the domes of St. Mark's Basilica, (below) the Clock Tower and the « Old Procuratie ».

ST. MARK'S BASILICA

This monument contains within it the complete political, social, and religious history of the Republic. Its origin dates back to 829 when the Doge Giustignano Partecipazio had it built to hold the mortal remains of St. Mark the Evangelist who had become the patron saint of the city. In 927 the basilica was destroyed by fire but was rebuilt in its actual architectural form between 1043 and 1071 by the Doge Domenico Contarini.

The building follows the scheme of byzantine churches, with the plan of a Greek cross and a dome, but it is interpreted in a romanesque style. The earlier solemn nakedness of the basilica's interior was soon forgotten with the execution of the very beautiful mosaic decoration, the precious marbles, and the architectural elements coming from the Orient; so that in it, the byzantine, gothic, islamic, and renaissance styles are all represented. The great golden basilica has become a complex masterpiece of art, thanks to the illustrious artists and fine Venetian craftsmen who helped to decorate it.

A scenic view of the **principal façade** which is 51.80 meters long. The five romanesque style entrances have internal oblique arches which are logically joined
together by the larger dominant arches. These are nobly interrupted by a narrow
balustrade, enlivened by spirited horses, and subdued by the fascinating Oriental
spires and domes. The entire façade is embellished by a rich marble decoration
and by splendid mosaics in the portals and arches. The three tall bronze pylons
in front of the basilica, on which the banners of the Republic were hoisted in
the past, are precious works by the goldsmith and sculptor Alessandro Leopardi
who executed them in 1505.

41

« **Carrying the body of St. Mark** » a mosaic of 1260-70.

« **The Venetians paying homage to the body of St. Mark** » by L. Ricci, 1728.

THE MOSAICS OF THE LUNETTES OVER THE ENTRANCES

« **The arrival of the body of St. Mark in Venice** » by P. Vecchia, 1660.

« **Stealing the body of St. Mark in Alexandria in Egypt** » by P. Vecchia, 1660.

The **principal portal** of the façade with the « **Universal Judgement** » by L. Querena, 1836.

The Deposition of Christ.

The Descent into Limbo.

THE MOSAICS OF THE SPIRES. - Executed by A. Gaetano, after drawings by Maffeo da Verona, between 1617 and 1618.

The Resurrection of Christ.

The Ascension of Christ.

The **large central spire** of the façade is a masterpiece of Tuscan sculptural art. St. Mark the Evangelist and the angels which rise towards him are by the Florentine Niccolò Lamberti who executed this work at the beginning of 1400.

In front of the large central window of the upper façade one can admire the **Four Horses** in gilded copper. They come from Constantinople and were plundered in the war of the Doge Enrico Dandolo during the Fourth Crusade in 1204. The four horses were placed here in the mid-fourteenth century. They appealed to Napoleon who brought them to Paris on December 17, 1797. They were returned to Venice in 1815.

THE INTERIOR OF ST. MARK'S BASILICA. - The sumptuous interior of the basilica has conserved the byzantine architectonic structure dating from the time of the Doge Contarini. It has a central plan in the form of a Greek cross, with a large central nave and a raised presbytery. The arms of the cross contain the minor naves. They are divided by pilasters and columns which support the womens' gallery.

Round arches, resting on angular columns, are

solid supports for the five domes. Originally, the walls and pilasters didn't have any marble decoration. This was added in 1159 with various precious materials for the most part, brought back from civil and religious buildings of the Orient and from Dalmatia. At the same time, the splendid mosaic decoration of the basilica was begun which has made it deserve the description « golden basilica ».

The columns, capitals, and parapets are all elements of high artistic value which give evidence of the taste and skill of the byzantine marble workers who carried out their work between the third and the thirteenth centuries. The rich pavement with various geometric designs and figures of animals dates from the twelfth century. It is a beautiful example of the art of marble mosaic. At the center, in front of the iconostasis, there is a large square of veined Greek marble, which in the past, the Venetians called the « sea » because of its waves.

THE MOSAICS OF THE BASILICA. - The charm and suggestion of the interior of the basilica is almost entirely due to the immense narrative in mosaic which runs along the walls, the vaults, and the dome, and which covers an area of more than four thousand square meters. This narrative cycle was begun in the eleventh century during the period of the Doge Domenico Selvo who governed the Republic between 1071 and 1084. It was continued during a second phase of work from the twelfth century to the end of the thirteenth century.

The byzantine mosaics were so rich and of such keen interest that a prodigious group of artists and technicians came to Venice. At the end of the eleventh century, they formed a flowering Venetian school which was largely influenced by the one in Ravenna. After a period of training and perfection, the Venetian school developed an artistic expression all its own. The fruits of this expression took place in the twelfth and thirte-

enth centuries during the growth of romanesque architecture. Further progress took place in the fourteenth century when mosaic decoration was inspired by traditional Venetian painting.

The decline of the art of mosaic began during the renaissance. To try to bring back its popularity the Procurators of the Republic called Paolo Uccello and Andrea del Castagno from Florence; thus, the passion for Venetian mosaic was renewed and in the sixteenth century some of the greatest artists of the time worked on cartoons for mosaic decoration: Titian, Lorenzo Lotto, Tintoretto, Veronese, Piazzetta, Salviati and Bassano.

Of the magnificent mosaics of the basilica we present here a series of beautiful details by masters of the fourteenth century.

1) **JESUS ARRIVES IN JERUSALEM**
2) **CHRIST ENTHRONED**
3-4) **THE MIRACLE OF ST. MARK**
5) **ST. JOHN THE EVANGELIST**
6) **ST. MARK THE EVANGELIST**
7) **ST. MATTHEW THE EVANGELIST**
8) **ST. LUKE THE EVANGELIST**
9) **JESUS IN THE GARDEN**

DUX

EKA
DIOS SUPRA
ATER
GASE

5

SIC ACTVS CHRISTI
SCT   MAEV

7

8

9

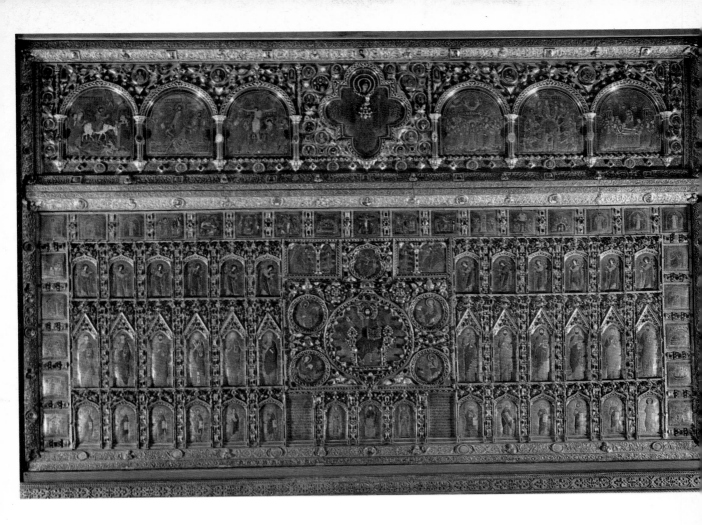

THE GOLDEN ALTAR-PIECE. - On the table of the principal altar, under which is kept the body of St. Mark, we find a real masterpiece of mediaeval goldsmith's work, called the Pala d'Oro (Golden Altar-piece). Its earlier form was begun in 978 when the Doge Pietro Orseolo gave the commission to some artists from Constantinople. In 1105 the altar-piece was rebuilt; then, it was enriched with gold and precious byzantine enamels belonging to the Monastery of the Pantocrator in Constantinople and brought to Venice during the Fourth Crusade in 1204.

Even if the materials have an Oriental origin the workmanship is the fruit of the artistic sensitivity of the Venetian goldsmith Giampaolo Boninsegna who executed it in its present form in 1345. The admirable composition is 3.40 meters wide, 1.40 meters high, and contains eighty enamels representing episodes of the life of the Redeemer, the Virgin, and St. Mark. A myriad of diamonds, emeralds, rubies, and topazes give a third dimension to the angels, prophets, evangelists, and portraits of Oriental emperors.

A detail of the mosaic of the dome over the baptismal font: **An apostle in the act of baptizing.**

THE BAPTISTRY. - A marvellous view of the Baptistry which has had its present form since 1350 when the Doge Andrea Dandolo commissioned it. In the center we see the large baptismal font executed by Tiziano Mineo, Desiderio da Firenze and Francesco Segala (1545) who did the statue of St. John the Baptist in 1575. On the right the tomb of the Doge Andrea Dandolo in Venetian gothic style. It was executed by the De Sanctis family, sculptors of the fourteenth century. The mosaic work of the walls, vaults, and domes was carried out by Venetian masters of the fourteenth century. It represents episodes of the life of St. John the Baptist and the Infancy of Jesus. On the rear wall, the « Crucifixion » with a portrait of Andrea Dandolo; in the dome above the baptismal font « Christ sends the Apostles to proclaim the good news »; and around the figure of Christ the « Apostles in the act of baptizing the people of various countries ». In the pendentives, four Doctors of the Greek Church. The dome above the altar contains the mosaic « Christ in Glory » and in the pendentives the figures of the four Doctors of the Latin Church.

THE DUCAL PALACE

This imposing and marvellous palace is called « ducal » because the supreme head of the State resided here since the nineth century. It was begun in the time of the Doges Angelo and Giustignano Partecipazio. In a byzantine style, it was built on pre-existing Roman walls. This early building was destroyed by fire and rebuilt several times. Only in 1340 did it assume its actual structure which is an expression of that period in which gothic art triumphed. The architect of the palace is unknown, however, it is known that the stone-cutter Filippo Calendario, a certain Pietro Baseio « magister porthus Palacii novi », and one named Proto Enrico contributed to its construction. In any case, between 1400 and 1424, the facade overlooking the quay and the one facing the square were finished.

Florentine and Milanese artists worked on the decoration of the grandiose palace, but the major part of the decorative complex in the flamboyant gothic style was carried out by famous Venetian marbleworkers of the Bon family. This magnificent, imposing structure is one of the most unique examples in the world of architectural elegance and harmony. The extended arcade of the ground

floor forms the base for the long, graceful loggia which runs along the two sides. Above the loggia, the luminous façade in a poly-chrome geometric design, is divided by large windows and by a central balcony. Bringing the marvellous structure to a conclusion is a white crenellation which gives to the decorative whole the preciousness and light-ness of lacework. On the left-hand page is a panoramic view which takes in the entire palace; on the right we see the two façades in all their graceful magnificence.

The Ducal Palace: **The balcony** which overlooks the square is by pupils of Jacopo Sansovino. Above we see the symbol of Venice with the Doge Andrea Gritti. The modern refacing of the building is by U. Bottasso. At the top, the statue of « Justice » by Alessandro Vittoria.

The Ducal Palace: **The luminous façade** overlooks the wharf with an admirable balcony in the florid gothic style. It was constructed in 1404 by Jacobello and Pier Paolo Dalle Masegne. In 1575 it underwent a change and the statue of « Justice » by Alessandro Vittoria was added. The façade on this side is 71.50 meters long. In the foreground the **Ponte della Paglia** (Bridge of Straw) which crosses over the **Rio di Palazzo** where we find the third façade designed by the architect Antonio Rizzo (1430-98).

THE TETRARCHS. - At the angle of St. Mark's Basilica, near the entrance to the Ducal Palace, one can admire this unusual group of fourth century sculptures in porphyry from Egypt or Syria. They represent four warriors who embrace each other. These so-called Tetrarchs were colleagues during the Empire of Diocletian.

The Ducal Palace: **The « Porta della Carta »** (door of the papers) so called because in the past, scribes were found here who wrote out documents for presentation to the various offices of the Republic. The precious decoration in florid gothic taste was executed by Giovanni and Bartolomeo Bon in 1438. Of particular beauty are the figures of the « Virtues » which can be seen in the niches of the pilasters. In the tondo, above the three-mullioned window, is the bust of St. Mark the Evangelist, and at the very top the statue of Justice. Immediately above the door, the « Doge Francesco Foscari and the Winged Lion » sculpted by L. Ferrari (1885) to substitute a similar one destroyed in 1797.

The Ducal Palace: This celebrated sculptural group, the **Judgement of Solomon**, is found on the corner pilaster near the « Door of the Papers ». A work of beautiful sculptural effect, it is attributed to Nanni di Bartolo il Rosso and to the Florentine school of the Lamberti.

The Ducal Palace: **The Courtyard.** In the middle, the bronze well-curbs sculpted by Niccolò dei Conti (1556) and Alfonso Alberghetti (1559). To the right the large façade of the palace with the lower part in gothic style and the upper part in renaissance style. It is an architectural masterpiece by Antonio Rizzo (1483-98). In the background to the left is the Clock façade, a baroque work by the architect Bartolomeo Manopola (1614). To the right, one side of the Foscari Arch with the statue of F. Maria Primo della Rovere by the Florentine sculptor G. Bandini.

The Ducal Palace: The « **Staircase of the Giants** », a pleasing design by the architect Antonio Rizzo. It has been given this name because of the enormous statues of Mars and Neptune sculpted by Sansovino. At the top of these stairs the Doge was crowned as soon as he was elected, in the presence of the people and the dignitaries of the Republic. Also ambassadors and illustrious guests were received here.

The Ducal Palace The « **Golden Staircase** » by which one arrives at the ducal apartment and the rooms of the third floor. It has assumed this name because of the magnificent decoration in gilded stucco created by Alessandro Vittoria. The stairs were constructed after a design by Sansovino between 1523 and 1538. The frescoes of the ceiling are by G. B. Franco.

THE INTERIOR OF THE DUCAL PALACE

Famous masters of architecture, painting, sculpture, and a large group of minor artists, unparalleled artisans of marble and stone, wood-carvers, stucco-workers, and gilders, all contributed, through the centuries, to the enrichment of the Ducal Palace; such names as Gentile da Fabriano and Pisanello who in the fifteenth century centinued the pictorial cycles in the Hall of the Major Council; Bellini, Vivarini, Carpaccio, Titian, Paolo Veronese, and Tintoretto for the other rooms. One can imagine how splendid the large rooms of the marvellous palace must have been at the beginning of the sixteenth century.

The palace, however, underwent two disastrous fires, one on May 11, 1574 and the other on December 20, 1577. They destroyed the rooms of the College, the Senate, and the upper floors of the building which overlook the square and the quay. These calamities annihilated the work of the above-mentioned artists as well as the internal architecture. It was decided to restore whatever was possible and to rebuild the rest respecting the antique gothic structure. Antonio da Ponte directed the work, and not many years past before the architectural reconstruction and the pictorial decoration of the Room of the Great Council and the Voting Room were brought to a conclusion. All the reconstructed rooms were re-provided with precious furnishings; however, these furnishings have not remained intact until our time because of the revolutionary violence which took place during the political events of May 1797. An exasperated crowd assaulted the palace, destroying the symbols of the past, and ruining everything within reach.

Under French and Austrian domination, the palace was the headquarters for governmental and municipal offices with grave losses to its conservation. So that in 1874 a complete restoration was undertaken followed by others directed by the Superintendent of Monuments.

The Ducal Palace: **The Anticollege**, that is, the anti-chamber where high magistrates and illustrious personalities waited to be presented to the Doge. Here we can see a detail of the rich stucco decoration by Alessandro Vittoria and some allegorical paintings by Francesco Montemezzano. Over the door, sculptures by Vittoria; on the wall above the door « Pallas and Mars » by J. Tintoretto; next to the door « The Rape of Europa » by Paolo Veronese.

The Ducal Palace: **The College Room** so-called because the great personalities of the Republic, presided over by the Doge, assembled in this room. They dealt with the affairs of State and they gave hearings to the ambassadors. The architecture is by Palladio (1573). On the beautiful ceiling pictorial masterpieces by Paolo Veronese. On the wall over the tribune « The Victory of Lepanto » by Veronese; on the right-hand wall in the background « The Mystical Marriage of St. Catherine » by Domenico Tintoretto; and on the near wall, the « Doge Niccolò da Ponte Invokes the Virgin » by J. Tintoretto.

The Ducal Palace: **The Senate Room** where the senators assembled presided over by the Doge. The pictorial cycle which decorates the walls and ceiling deals with the glorification of divine favour towards the Republic. The room was reconstructed by Antonio da Ponte. The ceiling, rich with very precious gilded carving by Cristoforo Sorte, also contains the great painting by Tintoretto called « The Triumph of Venice ». There are mythological figures in the oval paintings by T. Dolabella. On the wall with the throne, « The Doge Adoring the Dead Christ » by Jacopo Tintoretto. On the left-hand wall beyond the clock « Allegory of the League of Cambray Against Venice » by Jacopo Palma the Younger, and next to it the « Celebration of the Doge Pasquale Cicogna » by the same artist.

The Ducal Palace: **The Room of the Council of Ten.** Here, the highly feared magistrates assembled to investigate crimes of a political nature against the security of the State. The pictorial cycle decorating the room represents the endowments that should have inspired the conduct of the Council. On the left-hand wall « Pope Alessandro III, the Barbarossa and the Doge Ziani » by Francesco Leandro da Ponte; on the right-hand wall « The Adoration of the Magi » by Aliense. On the ceiling « Jupiter Attacks the Vices » a nineteenth century copy of a work by Veronese which is found in the Louvre.

The Ducal Palace: **The Room of the Bussola.** In the foreground the double door called the « Bussola » after which the room is named. It was here that the condemned and accused waited for decisions on their crimes against the security of the Republic. On the ceiling « St. Mark Crowns the Theological Virtues » a copy of the painting by Veronese now in the Louvre; on the right-hand wall « The Carmagnole Conquer Bergamo » by Aliense.

The Ducal Palace: In the Room of the Scudieri (equerry) one may admire this easel work by G. B. Tiepolo, « Neptune offers Venice the gifts of the sea ». It is one of the most significant canvases by the great master.

The Ducal Palace: **The Room of the Three Heads of the Council of Ten.** On the ceiling « The Victory of Virtue over Vice » by G. B. Zelotti. The large fireplace was built after a design by Sansovino by his pupils Pietro Grazioli da Salò and Danese Cattaneo. This room was used by the three magistrates selected to dispatch the corrispondence and to summon the reunions of the Council.

The Ducal Palace: **The Room of the Major Council.** Here, meetings were held by the highest Venetian magistrates who competed over the exercise of power. The room is 54 meters long, 25 meters wide and 15.40 meters high. Destroyed by fire in 1557, it was rebuilt by Antonio da Ponte and decorated with subjects suggested by the erudite Florentine Girolamo de' Bardi and the Venetian historian F. Sansovino. The pictorial decoration celebrates the glories of the Republic. Above the tribune, the grandiose canvas by Tintoretto called « Paradise ». On the ceiling, in the large rectangle « Venice among the gods receives homage from her subject people » by Jacopo Tintoretto.

The Ducal Palace: **The Voting Room** was rebuilt by Antonio da Ponte after the fire of 1577. Girolamo de' Bardi suggested subjects for the pictorial decoration of the ceiling and walls which exalt the marine glories of the Republic. In the background the Arch of Triumph by A. Tirali constructed in 1694 to honor the Doge Francesco Morosini for the Peloponnesian Conquest. On the right-hand wall « The Battle of Lepanto » by A. Vicentino, and after the door « The Victory of the Dardanelles » by Pietro Liberi.

THE ISLAND OF SAN GIORGIO MAGGIORE. - In front of the Piazzetta (the smaller square connected to St. Mark's Square), one can see this scenic island surrounded by the sea. In the past, it was called the Island of the Cypresses. The Benedictine Monks resided there until 982. The convent is now the headquarters of the Giorgio Cini Foundation, an International Center of Culture and Art. Cosimo de' Medici the Elder resided there during his exile in 1433. (For a description of the church, see page 113).

A view of the animated **Riva degli Schiavoni** (Bank of the Slavonians) which offers one of the most beautiful walks you may take in Venice. It was named after the Dalmatian merchants from Slavonia who moored their ships here.

THE BRIDGE OF SIGHS. - This charming suspended construction passes over the Rio di Palazzo. In baroque style, it is by the architect Antonio Contino (1599). It connects the Ducal Palace with the Prisons. Once prisoners crossed over the bridge to appear before the judges. The only moment in which they were able to see the lagoon was when they passed in front of the open-work windows, and they probably sighed for their lost liberty.

A row of gondolas moored to the tract of land which goes from **Rio di Palazzo** to **Rio del Vin.** Next to the Ducal Palace is the former Prison constructed between 1589 and 1614; then, the Hotel Danieli which also includes the **Dandolo Palace** of the fifteenth century.

This photograph, taken from the royal gardens of the former Prison, takes in the entire political, civil, and religious center of the Republic.

Two characteristic narrow streets near St. Mark's Square.

A STROLL THROUGH VENICE

Looking at the city only from the Grand Canal, or from the center of St. Mark's Square gives the visitor an incomplete picture of this queen of the Adriatic. If one really wants to enjoy to the full the many picturesque, charming, and artistic things which are hidden, one must not be afraid to get lost in the labyrinth of canals and squares. Only in this way will we discover, district by district, the great wealth of works of art; the splendour of the palaces and churches; the sequence of curious light effects in the canals which are reflected on the architecture and on the more humble living quarters. Frequently we see clothes hung out to dry in the sun, bird cages, and vases of flowers, all of which help to create an atmosphere of festive serenity.

Above all, strolling around, one is able to have contact with the genuine Venetian people who are so kind and sincere, ready to be useful if you are having difficulty finding your way, and they will put at your ease. Only after having had this experience are we able to carry away with us the unforgettable memory of this unique city.

The gondolas glide lightly and silently along the picturesque Rio di Palazzo which ends at the quay and surrounds the Ducal Palace.

In the district of Castello the very beauitful **Church of San Zaccaria** facing a square which bears the same name. The church dates back to the tenth century, but was reconstructed between 1470 and 1500 by the architects Antonio Gambello and Mauro Codussi who gave it this magnificent façade with six orders. It is a true masterpiece of the Venetian renaissance. Above the portal, the statue of San Zaccaria by Alessandro Vittoria. On both sides of the portal, figures of the prophets within renaissance frames.

In the district of Dorsoduro the **Church of San Barnaba** built in 1749 by the architect Lorenzo Boschetti. It has a classical type façade, with Corinthian columns and a tympanum. The beautiful bell tower is in the romanesque style.

Two panoramic views of the characteristic roofs of Venice. Above, we can see in the background the Church of San Giovanni and Paolo and the Scuola Grande di San Marco.

The San Moisé Canal passes in front of the church bearing the same name. It empties into the Grand Canal between the Tiepolo Palace and the Treves dei Bonfili Palace.

The Church of San Moisé, dating from the eighth century was built to honor San Vittore. It seems that it was reconstructed in the tenth century by a certain Moisé Venier who gave it the name of this patron saint. The façade, in a picturesque baroque style, is by A. Tremignon and A. Meyring (1668). In the church, there is the tomb of Giovanni Law (1729), who was the first to introduce paper money into the banking system.

In the District of Castello, we find the square called **Santa Maria Formosa.** It is rich with noteworthy artistic buildings, among them the Church of Santa Maria Formosa. The origin of the church dates back to the seventh century. It was founded to honor the Virgin who appeared as a stately matron, and was named after Her. Reconstructed after a plan by the architect Mauro Codussi in 1492, it has two sixteenth century façades: one overlooking a canal, and the other facing the square. The first façade dates back to 1542, the second, which you see here, is of 1604. On the façade there are three portraits of members of the Casa Cappello family who provided the means for it's construction. At the top there are five seventeenth century statues of « The Virgin among the Virtues ». The bell tower is in the baroque style.

One of the many characteristic and picturesque Venetian canals which penetrate into the most hidden heart of the city.

In the imposing **Square of San Giovanni and Paolo**, in the District of Castello, the equestrian statue of the condottiere **Bartolomeo Colleoni** stands, dominating the surroundings. A masterpiece by the Florentine sculptor Andrea del Verrocchio, it was cast by the Venetian sculptor and caster Alessandro Leopardi who is responsible for the rich and beautiful base of the statue.

The Domenican **Church of San Giovanni and Paolo** is a fine example of Venetian gothic architecture begun in 1246 and finished in 1430. It is the Pantheon of Venetian glories because here are found the tombs of those who deserved the recognition of the Venetian Republic. On the unfinished brick façade is the beautiful portal, a rare combination of gothic and renaissance elements. It is attributed to Antonio Gambello.

95

A popular tradition tells us that the **Church of San Giacomo di Rialto** is the oldest in Venice. It dates back to the eleventh and twelfth centuries. The curious façade with a charming gothic portico is dominated by the large clock constructed in 1410. Under the small bell tower is a gothic relief of the « Madonna and Child ».

Another characteristic view of the Venetian interior: the **Rio del Vin** (Canal of Wine).

Along the Rio dei Mendicanti (Canal of the Beggars) in the Square of San Giovanni and Paolo we find the harmonious **Scuola Grande di San Marco**, which is now the Civil Hospital. It is a masterpiece of Renaissance architecture by Pietro Lombardo and Mauro Coduzzi. The sculptures on the façade are by Bartolomeo Bon and T. Lombardo. The building was executed between 1485 and 1495.

San Bartolomeo Square is one of the most lively centers of the city because the canals coming from St. Mark's, Cannaregio, Castello, and Rialto Bridge all converge here. In the center of the square is a monument to Carlo Goldoni, the ingenious playwright who represented so many aspects of contemporary Venetian life in his witty theatrical works. His statue is by the sculptor Antonio Dal Zotto and was unveiled in 1883.

Another splendid view of the structure of Rialto Bridge.

The picturesque fruit and vegetable market along the street called Ruga degli Orefici at the foot of the Rialto Bridge.

Cannaregio Canal. - One of the principal and very busy waterways which connect the Grand Canal to the lagoon.

Fine Venetian cooking may be tried at many of the city's restaurants. Cooks are expert in preparing dishes with fresh Adriatic fish; such specialities as « granseola », « canestrelli in umido », « folpetto all'olio », and « baccalà alla vicentina ».

A detail of large **San Paolo Square** in which we see the following palaces: Tiepolo, Soranzo, Donà, and Corner-Mocenigo. Being the most spacious square in Venice, meetings of the people, celebrations, bull hunts, weekly fairs, and military parades were held here.

SANTA MARIA GLORIOSA DEI FRARI. - This church is found in the District of San Paolo near Ca' Grande. It is the most important architectural structure in the Venetian-gothic style after St. Mark's Basilica. It was built between 1340 and 1443 for the Order of Frati Minori di S. Francesco. It seems that Fra Scipione Bon was the architect. Like the church of San Giovanni and Paolo, it contains the tombs of illustrious personages of the Republic and numerous masterpieces of art. The austere and imposing façade is divided by pilasters. Over the door a « Blessed Christ » by A. Vittoria, and a « Madonna » and « St. Francis » by B. Bon.

Santa Maria Gloriosa dei Frari: The very famous masterpiece the « **Assumption** » by Titian, is found at the center of the presbytery. The grandiose canvas is 6.50 meters high and 3.60 meters wide.

The incomparable stately **interior of Santa Maria Gloriosa dei Frari.** Twelve pillars with wooden beams divide the space into three naves. The ceiling has vaults with acute arches. At the center is the choir with beautiful sculptures by Bon and Lombardo.

Two minor views of characteristic urban settings in Venice with houses and palaces reflected in the canals.

The Church of San Rocco contains the body of this French saint who during his life was dedicated to curing the sick. The church was begun in 1489 and finished in the eighteenth century. The façade, which was inspired by the work of Codussi in the nearby School of San Rocco, is by the architect B. Maccaruzzi who designed it between 1765 and 1771. In the lunette of the doorway a bronze reproduction of a pre-existent marble relief « San Rocco carried by the angels to the sky » by G. Marchiori. The statues of San Pietro Orseolo and San Gherardo Safredo are by the same artist. In the upper section of the façade, the central panel depicts « San Rocco assisting the sick », and at the sides the statues of San Lorenzo Giustiniani and the Blessed Gregorio Barbarigo. Crowning the façade « San Rocco between St. Pietro Acotanto and Jacopo Salomonio », all by the sculptor G. M. Morleiter.

Nearby **San Trovaso Square** (St. Gervasio and Protasio) in the District of Dorsoduro is the San Trovaso Canal where we find this picturesque view of a « squero »,
a dockyard for the building and repairing of gondolas. Venice once had many
of these dockyards. Here, we see an example of how they were built of wood,
while the lower class houses were built of brickwork. Behind, is the Church of
San Trovaso, existing since the eleventh century. It was rebuilt in the Palladian
style in 1584.

A picturesque view of the **San Barnaba Canal** which flows into the Grand Canal
going around the Rezzonico Palace.

The **San Trovaso Canal** is a lively waterway which joins the Grand Canal to the Giudecca Canal.

The **San Vito Canal** is between the Grand Canal and the Giudecca Canal.

This curious Lombard **spiral staircase** may be admired from the adjoining courtyard of the Contarini Dal Bovolo Palace. It was executed in 1500 by Giovanni Candi.

The spacious **Santo Stefano Square** with a monument to Niccolò Tommaseo by the sculptor Francesco Barzaghi (1882). Here we see only a small section of the square, but along its perimeter are found the Churches of San Vitale and San Stefano, and the Franchetti, Pisani, and Loredan Palace. In antique times, the square was a theatre of bull hunting.

The white Palladian **Church of San Giorgio** and the antique Benedictine Convent which now belongs to the Cini Foundation, are on the Island of San Giorgio Maggiore. Andrea Palladio created this beautiful church which was begun and finished between 1565 and 1610. The bell tower collapsed in 1773 and was rebuilt in 1791 by the Bolognese architect Benedetto Buratti.

The grandiose and animated **Giudecca Canal**, abundant with dockyards and factories, is seen here from the Island of San Giorgio Maggiore. There are two theories about the origin of its name: Hebrews or Jews (giudei) were once confined to this quarter, therefore the name Giudecca; the second theory is that the name derives from « Zudegà » meaning « the judged ones » because in the nineth century the nobility in revolt were confined to live here.

THE ENVIRONS OF VENICE

THE LIDO OF VENICE. - An island with an elongated form, the Lido was an antique defense rampart for the city. In modern times, it has become an internationally famous seaside resort because of its well-equipt hotel accommodations for tourists, its beautiful beach, and its cultural, artistic, and sporting manifestations which are held during the summer season.

THE ISLAND OF MURANO: Originally it was calledAmurianum and is one of the largest islands of the Venetian lagoon. Also, like Venice, it is made up of several smaller islands, intersected by canals with bridges, foundations and smaller canals. It dates back perhaps to the tenth century, was governed

The **Grand Canal of Murano** cuts across the entire island. Once a year, a famous regata takes place on this canal.

The apse of the **Basilica of Santa Maria and Donato** in the Venetian-byzantine style of the twelfth century.

autonomously, had the right to its own nobility and the privilege of coining the so-called "oselle" or souvenir-money for the elections of the Doges of Venice. It flourished eminently because of its numerous industries and its proximity to the Republic. It reached its maximum splendour in the sixteenth century, especially for the development of the art of glass-making.

Murano is famous for its glass-makers. **The art of glass-making** dates back to 1289. It flourished in the fifteenth and sixteenth century, and acquired new value in the eighteenth century with the introduction of new techniques. It declined in the last century, but today has returned to its ancient splendour with an artisan production of high artistic level. In the photograph, a phase of glass-making.

THE ISLAND OF BURANO: It owes its foundation to the inhabitants of Altino who in the fifth century escaped from the invasion of Attila. A characteristic cadence in the dialect of the people has been conserved from this distant origin. There are several things worth visiting on the island: the sixteenth century parish church of San Martino with vaulted ceiling has the form of a Latin cross and is divided into three naves; among the

In the photograph: a picturesque area of the island which is greatly admired by painters because of the blending and contrast of its colors.

several works of art, there is a grandiose «Crucifixion» by Giambattista Tiepolo executed about 1725. The great musician Baldassarre Galuppi called Buranello was born on the Island of Burano (1703-85).

BURANO LACE-WORK. - This antique island is even more famous for its exquisite artistic « merletti » (lace-work), an industry which has given it an enviable economic prosperity. These hand-made articles, executed entirely with the needle, have captured the taste of women from all over the world because of their delicateness and large variety of stitches. Burano lace was already known in the fifteenth century. In the following century, Catherine de' Medici, Queen of France, who was also an accomplished embroideress, patronized this fine art by enriching it with the designs of skilled Italian artists.

THE ISLAND OF TORCELLO: Also this island, which in antique times was called New Altino, dates back to the period between the fifth and sixth century when the Huns and the Longobards invaded and partly destroyed the Altino. In the seventh century it was under the Byzantine Empire; it became the episcopal seat and one of the most important commercial centers of the lagoon with a population of about twenty thousand inhabitants. Its prosperity began to decline with

In the photograph: a detail of the beautiful Island of Torcello taken from the landing-place.

the assertion of Venetian power and with the spread of malaria which in a short time depopulated it. Today it has become a small fishing center and is of great historic and artistic interest. It is named after an antique tower, « turricellum », built to ward off enemy attacks.

THE ISLAND OF TORCELLO: On the left the most important monument on the island, the **Cathedral of Santa Maria Assunta**; on the right the beautiful Church of Santa Fosca. The byzantine style cathedral was founded in 639, but underwent modifications in 864 and 1008. The construction of the imposing bell tower dates back to the eleventh century. The interior of the cathedral has a basilical plan, and is divided into three naves. On the walls of the entrance is a grandiose and beautiful mosaic of the twelfth century depicting the « Universal Judgement ». The mosaic decoration which continues along the walls represents other subjects. The **Church of Santa Fosca**, in the style of Ravenna, was rebuilt in the eleventh century. The exterior has an harmonious arcade supported by white marble columns, and a pentagonal apse. The interior, in the form of a Greek cross, is transformed from a square form to a circular one because of the program to eventually add a dome which was never executed. The entire church is very interesting from the architectural point of view.

THE GONDOLA: Made famous by poets, musicians, and writers, this characteristic and elegant boat constitutes an indispensable element of Venetian tourism. Its name, according to the « Venetian Lexicon », derives from « cymbula » (small boat). In antique times the letter « y » was pronounced like a « u », and often the Venetians changed the « c » to a « g ». So the word « gundula » was born, which then became « gondola ». The origin of the gondola is very antique. It seems to date back to the eleventh century. Its form was different than it is today; being much longer, it was manoeuvred by twelve oarsmen. In the renaissance, it became smaller; it was eleven meters long and 1.40 meters wide. Decorated richly and sumptuously in the sixteenth and seventeenth century, it was simplified in the nineteenth century. The technique of building a gondola is quite complicated; it is composed of two hundred and eighty pieces of wood of several different types. With all its metal finishings, etc., it weighs about 1500 pounds.

I N D E X

Finito di stampare in Firenze nel Febbraio 1972